AWAKENING COMMUNITY INTELLIGENCE

CSA Farms as 21st Century Cornerstones

by Steven McFadden

Copyright © 2015
Soul*Sparks Books
An imprint of Light and Sound Press, LLC

Light and Sound Press, LLC
www.lightandsoundpress.com

Awakening Community Intelligence
Create Space edition 1.2
ISBN-13: 978-1512158359

For twin brother
Michael Dennis McFadden
(1948-2015)

CONTENTS

ACKNOWLEDGMENTS

Many people have earned our respect and gratitude for their influence, for their sophisticated insights, and for their support. We note especially the farmers and families of the Temple-Wilton Community Farm, and the many diligent stewards of the earth who have been our neighbors in Nebraska and across the Americas.

I thank my Muse and my partner in life, in love, and in Soul*Sparks Books: Elizabeth Wolf. Great thanks also to the many farmers and earth patriots of the world–the wide-ranging communities of human beings who originated the models of food co-ops and Community Supported Agriculture (CSA), and who continue to cultivate them. Their plentiful insights are woven into this e-book. Our gratitude to one and all.

~ SM

Cover photo by curiouslee via flickr (Creative Commons)

~ INTRODUCTION ~

Over the last decades many thousands of people in all parts of the world have come to recognize in Community Supported Agriculture (CSA) a vehicle for approaching land, food, labor, environment and community in a healthier way. Now – in an era with increasing shadows of environmental catastrophe – it's time to expand exponentially the CSA vision and reality. The opportunity is before us.

CSA is a social and economic arrangement in which specific communities – neighborhoods, churches, workplaces, and so forth – willingly share responsibility with specific farmers for producing, delivering, enjoying and honoring the food that sustains them. The community supports the farm, and the farm supports the community.

In theory and generally in practice, the associations integral to CSA foster mutual respect. CSA has thus emerged as a dynamic pathway directly linking human beings and their communities in free-will association with nearby farms and the farmers who touch the earth on their behalf. These farmers may rightly be regarded as our ambassadors to the earth. Rather than making war on nature, they strive to cooperate intelligently and thereby maintain respectful relations. They are making an important and positive difference in the world. Much more is necessary. Much more is possible.

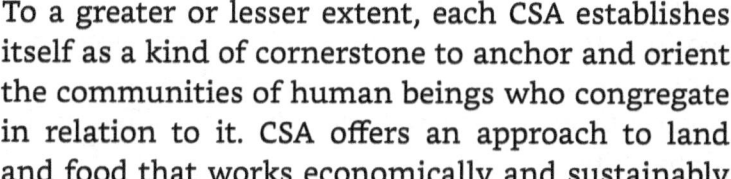

To a greater or lesser extent, each CSA establishes itself as a kind of cornerstone to anchor and orient the communities of human beings who congregate in relation to it. CSA offers an approach to land and food that works economically and sustainably in a host of situations, and thus can be further developed as a model for 21st century communities and the sophisticated networks they create within and among themselves.

As amply demonstrated across the Internet, CSA farms tend naturally to accomodate digital, high-tech advances, and skillfully to weave them into their webs of land, food and human beings. To the extent that a given CSA functions as a community cornerstone or touchstone, it has established a dynamic form that enables the community to focus its resources and strengths for a common good.

Our civilization is reckoning with profound disruptions associated with climate change, resource depletion and geopolitical instability. Of critical note, this year 30 of the world's largest insurance companies, known for their conservative approach in all matters, have established a formal coalition (SmarterSafer) to sound the alarm, and let people, corporations and governments know that we face increasingly extreme circumstances. It's going to be perilous and costly for everyone. Meanwhile, Standard & Poor's Rating Service, the world's foremost credit ranking company, has issued a report saying that credit ratings of sovereign countries will be adversely affected by global climate chaos.

These hard realities are indisputable. Only the willingly blind can fail to see the necessity of embarking now on a vigorous, wholehearted journey toward sustainability for home, community, nation, and planet. We must respond to our circumstances, or be overwhelmed.

Both globally and locally, we absolutely require intelligent strategies to reduce our vulnerability, to build resilience, and to reckon with the increasing disruptions of climate change and our pervasive pattern of planetary pollution and resource depletion. CSA farms stand out as promising models, models with a noteworthy track record. If the CSA model is in fact realized in hundreds of thousands of permutations in diverse communities around the globe, it can make a consequential difference in a host of sane, safe, and superior ways.

Our survival requires not just the intelligent actions

of individuals but also hundreds of thousands of communities of human beings who have had their inate intelligence awakened, and who thus realize the fundamental link between life and land. In this regard, Community Supported Agriculture (CSA) provides a useful and egalitarian model.

While not a full answer to the immediate challenges of our era, the CSA farm model has shown that it can be adapted to fit with a wide range of specific cultures and circumstances, and a variety of natural environments. CSA has in recent years been quietly, steadily establishing itself around the globe with a growing network of CSA cornerstones not just in the USA and Japan, but also in Canada, Australia, Ireland, France, Germany, England, Israel, South Korea, Egypt, China, Africa and many other locales.

In the craft of masonry the cornerstone is the beginning, the base from which other stones are set and the building takes its form. The cornerstone thus determines the orientation, cohesion, and strength of the whole structure. In appreciating this literal definition, I recognize also that my choice of cornerstone as a metaphor to try and convey a vision of what is necessary and possible with CSA in the 21st Century and beyond may seem improbable or awkward to some. But I see it as fitting.

While literal cornerstones are static blocks of

rock, CSA farms are dynamic organisms involving a congregation of human beings and the natural world. As such, CSAs have ever-changing ecological, social and economic characteristics, yet at the same time they serve to organize human beings and natural resources in a healthy and mutually beneficial association, and to orient them in positive directions. That statement describes an ideal, I realize. But ideals are a necessary element of vision, and vision is necessary before anyone – or any community – sets off in a given direction. It's time for us all – individuals, communities, and nations – to start moving in some new directions right now. CSA offers promising pathways that can be important for millions.

In the context of this book's central metaphor, the colorful image on the cover is intended to symbolize the general shape of a cornerstone, but a cornerstone vibrant with a network of life-giving light impulses. To me the image seems an apt visual metaphor for the ideals, the potential – and to a certain extent the current reality – of CSA at this still early stage of the 21st Century. Cornerstones – including CSA cornerstones – are something you can build upon.

With the benefit of three decades of involvement and observation, I've come to appreciate CSA as a

21st Century agrarian initiative with tremendous potential to organize human beings – out of their free-will choices – around the essential matter of a renewed relationship with the land that sustains us all, as well as renewed relationships with each other and our food.

Considering the global totality of our economic, environmental and social realities, something more is needed. Something profoundly different. That's the potential CSA has – the potential to be profoundly different by serving as a model for a dynamic, far-flung, and intelligent network of nodes: community cornerstones that orient and sustain natural communities of neighborhoods, churches, and workplaces.

For long centuries many parts of the world endured hierarchical social systems known as feudalism. The king or his equivalent had the top spot in the community and was supported by ranks of men who were granted an elite status. Massed below the elites were the peasants, or commoners. Based on raw power, claims of land ownership and the stoop labor of the commoners, feudalism channeled wealth systematically upwards into the hands of the 'elite.'

Since the advent of industrialism, systems of capitalism have evolved to supplant systems of feudalism. The owners of capital have formed their own executive aristocracy with rank predicated on net worth. Meanwhile latter-day commoners (*proles* in the parlance of Orwell's novel, *1984*) labor for wages. They are quietly entangled through debt to corporate institutions, and otherwise distracted from gross imbalances and injustices via stupefying quantities of alcohol and pharmaceuticals, supplemented by a nervous overwhelm of diverting infotainment.

This social arrangement is not a model or system that serves the toxic, turbulent and troubled present, nor can it serve the future. It's unbalanced and unsustainable. It also represents a tremendous loss of potential for the human spirit and for human freedom, as well as steady, ongoing despoilment of the earth we all depend upon for survival.

Variations on the hierarchical, overlord model likewise pervade the essential domains of agriculture and food, with increasing corporate monopolies and patents on seeds, chemicals, and credit. This trend has profound consequences for human livelihood, as well as for social equity, environmental sustainability, food quality, spiritual freedom and animal welfare.

In response to apparent, unsustainable realities, thousands of people in America and around the world — in community organizations, at universities, within local, state, tribal, church, and national agencies, and in businesses — are actively seeking better, healthier ways. They are asking what a sustainable food system could look like and how might we get there? They are continuing to bring forth a wealth of sustainable agrarian innovations. CSAs and networks of CSAs, I submit, can be an even more substantial part of this range of responses to the challenge of our times.

CSAs are non-hierarchal organisms that effectively awaken, activate and support healthy relationships among people, land, food, and culture. This we have seen evidenced in the growth of the model nationally and internationally. CSAs thus can serve the world's diverse communities as metaphorical, metaphysical, and material cornerstones.

On a mechanical level, *Awakening Community Intelligence* is in part a compilation and adaptation of articles I've written and published elsewhere over the years, and some new understandings. On the aspirational level, it's a more comprehensive expression of an evolving CSA vision in response to the extreme status of our natural and geopolitical worlds. Having beheld the vision, as have many others, I have written this book in an effort to advance the vision more coherently, and to explore also some of the urgently relevant social, economic and environmental elements of CSA.

When Trauger Groh and I coauthored two books on CSA (*Farms of Tomorrow: Community Supported Farms, Farm Supported Communities* in 1990, and *Farms of Tomorrow Revisited* in 1998), we offered the understanding that something new was necessary, not just because of economic and social inequities, but also because of the vast exploitation of the earth's resources at a stupendously destructive rate.

We wrote that farming is not just a business like any other profit-making business, but a precondition of all human life on earth, and a precondition of all economic activity. "As such," we wrote, "farming is everyone's responsibility, and has likewise to be accessible for everyone. The problems of agriculture and the environment belong not just to farmers, but are the common problems of all people."

In our 21st Century of ecological and climatological catastrophe, that basic fact makes new social, environmental and economic structures for farming essential. CSA addresses these fundamental matters directly and creatively. Thus, in the context of necessity, experience and possibility, it's time now to re-articulate the CSA vision and to advocate that it be embraced more widely as a way to establish useful and necessary community cornerstones.

Community farming is about the necessary renewal of agriculture through its healthy linkage with the human community that depends on farming for survival – a human community that engages with farming out of intelligence and free will, rather than corporate or governmental mandate or manipulation. CSA is also about the necessary stewardship of soil, plants, and animals: the essential capital of all human cultures.

As this early juncture of the 21st Century, such a thesis runs the risk of earning this volume critical condemnation as pie-in-the-sky *agrifantasy*. But then that's the sort of thing critics said when Trauger and I wrote *Farms of Tomorrow*. Back then, in 1990, there were only about 90 CSA farms. Now there may well be as many as 12,000 in the USA and growing, and many thousands more worldwide.

CSA is not fantasy. It is vision brought to life by communities of human beings all over the world. Likewise, the possibility of a global population of hundreds of thousands of CSA community cornerstones, many of them networked and associated, is not fantasy either. It's also vision – vision that arises from a wide, multicultural global community of intelligent human beings, and that is based on necessity, experience, and possibility.

Perhaps by the time we get to the 22nd Century

the concept of Community Supported Agriculture will have become quaint or irrelevant. Perhaps by then we human beings will have evolved a basic level of wisdom about our life-support systems: our water, land, food, and the farmers who touch the earth for us. Perhaps by then we will have awakened community and corporate responsibility for stewarding it all. Such realizations are devoutly to be wished.

But right now, in this still-early phase of our intensely distressed 21st Century, we do need CSA farms and we need hundreds of thousands more of them. CSAs and CSA networks can serve as healing and strengthening cornerstones for communities through an era of essential transformation. They can anchor networks of human beings to the land in a matrix of healthy, supportive relationships with plants, animals and soil, and orient them in positive directions. Such community cornerstones represent intelligence in action.

~ *Chapter 1* ~
Awakening Community Intelligence

The Food and Agriculture Organization (FAO) of the United Nations has declared definitively that the world must turn swiftly from radically polluting, petroleum-based industrial agricultural practices and move actively toward sustainable systems. They term this approach to farming *agroecology*, and they define it as agriculture that focuses not only on production, but also – based on both common sense and mounds of scientific evidence – on ecological sustainability.

Clean, non-toxic approaches to growing food, such as are employed at CSA farms, have a solid track record for economic, environmental and dietary excellence. As demonstrated in comprehensive studies from the FAO, from Rodale Institute, and from other research organizations, agroecological farming can supply all the clean food necessary to feed the world. And it can do this while improving soil, air, and water quality, helping to stabilize Earth's climate by sequestering carbon, and by enhancing physical and mental health for human beings.

This kind of land-based wisdom needs to be near the heart of our individual, community, and planetary efforts to cope with climate chaos. CSA farms are one natural way to bring agroecological approaches into wider practice, a basic act of intelligence for any group of individuals or any form of community.

The local food movement – whether centered in a CSA, a co-op or a farmers market – is no fad or whim, but is driven by acutely realistic economic, environmental and health concerns. For a host of compelling reasons, there is a growing understanding that good food and a clean, non-toxic environment are foundational, and must be in a mutually respectful and beneficial relationship.

Because CSA possesses so many inherently beneficial dimensions, I continue to regard CSAs as a way of building a clean, stable agrarian foundation for the fast emerging high-tech digital-wave culture. The digital culture can in reciprocity connect, network and sustain the agrarian initiatives which give it roots. In this regard the element of community is just as important as the practical and economic arrangements that take place in a CSA.

The dynamic of farmers and consumers in free will association via community farms creates the potential for the kind of phenomenon that philosopher Rudolf Steiner termed "social intelligence." In the particular case of CSA, that construct naturally extends to include economic and environmental intelligence as well.

Rather than an agriculture that is supported by government subsidies, private profits, or martyrs to the cause, CSA pioneers envisioned organizational forms that provide direct, free will support for farm and farmers from the people who share in the harvest they have made possible.

As Trauger has noted, "That farms flourish must be the concern of everyone, not just the individuals working as farmers." The idea is for the community to support the whole farm, not just to be occasional consumers buying boxes of carrots, lettuce, and strawberries. When CSA shareholders support the whole farm, the farm is in better position to reciprocate and to support the community. The community supports the farm out of free will association, and the farm supports the community out of the bounty of the land.

Writing in the journal *Biodynamics,* Jeff Poppen observed that CSA has its roots in the recognition of the fundamental difference between growing something and selling something. "When a group of people cover the farm's annual budget, as in CSA," Poppen wrote, "the farmer is able to put all his or her attention into developing the farm's unique possibilities..."

The core ideas of CSA – the sparks that have defined

it and made it so immediately understandable and appealing for people – are about supporting a whole farm, and having the whole farm support and nourish the web of people who support it. Ultimately, this is what makes a CSA a CSA.

By supporting the whole farm rather than just buying some food the farm has produced, shareholders are more fully invested and involved. They come to know the full scope of what their investment and participation are accomplishing.

As outlined in *The Big Disconnect: Protecting Childhood and Family Relationships in the Digital Age* by Catherine Steiner-Adair and Teresa Barker, today's generations of children are by and large growing up indoors, with far less time spent in nature or out of doors. Technology is efficiently, mechanistically drawing people into private and separate worlds. The constant high-intensity pulses of the digital realm can overwhelm or short-circuit organic nervous systems. This distancing from the natural world has consequences for individuals and society. Plugged-in existence is a fact of modern life, not likely soon to cease.

For people of all ages an increasingly common outcome is a sense of detachment, what social scientists identify as "disembeddedness" from the world. Increasingly the natural world – the earth itself, the air, the trees, the realms of animals, plants, oceans, deserts and mountains – are becoming more of an abstract concept and less of a daily reality. That's dangerous. It's physically dangerous, but it's also dangerous psychologically and spiritually.

Lakota philosopher Luther Standing Bear long ago made a trenchant observation about this: "...a man's heart, away from nature, becomes hard. Lack of respect for living, growing, things soon leads to lack of respect for humans as well..." This caution merits respectful attention.

Our lives are undergoing a massive transformation of many dimensions at this early stage of the 21st Century. In the vortex of this change, community farm cornerstones can provide key points of stability and orientation, and a bushel basket of benefits: physical, emotional, psychological, social, and environmental. It's good to fly high and explore the uncharted reaches of life and the world, but it's wisest to do so with a steadying home base cornerstone. In that sense, it's also good to be grounded.

~ *Chapter 2* ~
Creating a Future

After three decades of development in North America many CSAs face challenging questions around the actual definition and expression of community in their 21st Century agrarian initiatives. What does the "community" part of CSA really mean? Is CSA going to be subsumed as just another "business model" based primarily on monetary transactions for food from vaguely known consumers? Or will it – as it has the potential – become a model for fully healthy cells of social well-being, environmental health, and economic justice?

As a longtime CSA shareholder and reporter, I've always hypothesized that over time in eras of economic stress, CSA social networks would assume increasing importance. That's because through CSA individuals, households, and farmers have direct opportunity to form a wide constellation of relationships. They can support and feed each other on a lot of levels. They are linked not just by theories of the ideal, but also by matters that are inescapably real: land, farms and food, as well as personal well-being, family, and community health.

Yet many farmers and CSA shareholders identify community as a weak part of CSA. They say that it just is not happening as theorized. The realm of the ideal has had a hard reckoning with the realm of the real.

In taking up the subject of community in CSA, I also had to reckon with reality. I'm a journalist, not a scholar. I've not conducted any new research studies for this book. Rather, I've reviewed what I have learned over my decades of interest and participation in CSA, weighed that with the observations and ideas that I've heard others express, and also considered the insights presented in a range of scholarly and popular books and articles on CSA.

What is working well in building and sustaining community? There are a multitude of dimensions, involving topics as diverse as motivation, social structure, mutual association, virtual association, core groups, networking, conflict resolution, long-term commitment, and social intelligence. That's a lot of territory, but it all relates to community – the core construct that makes it possible for the emergence of these agrarian initiatives known as CSA.

If there is a common understanding among people who have been involved with CSAs, it is that there isn't a canned formula. Each group that gets started has to assess its own goals, skills and resources, and then proceed from that point – working with what is available to reach toward the goals the farmers and shareholders choose.

Having proven itself in general, CSA has over time branched into a range of creative permutations, including neighborhood CSAs, faith-based CSAs, workplace CSAs, community-kitchen focused CSAs, and CSAs focused on fruit, seafood, eggs, meat, wine and other provisions. No doubt the innovations, permutations and associations will continue to evolve over time.

Likewise, over time each CSA farm forms (or malforms) its own particular social constellations.

This first half of the 21st Century is a moment in time when, prompted by basic common sense, more people are looking to become active in creating a sustainable future.

Anthropologists Cynthia Abbott Cone, Ann Kakaliouras and Andrea Myhre have collaborated on a number of papers on CSA. In their studies they note that Anthony Gidden's conceptions concerning the dilemmas of modernity (*Modernity and Self-Identity*), help to explain the commitment of many CSA farmers and shareholders, particularly those who are long-term and highly active. The most oft-articulated reason for joining a CSA they encountered: the quality of food and environment.

But shareholder interviews suggest that participation in farm activities is also closely tied to a sense of civic responsibility and spiritual fulfillment. In fact, the farm studied with the highest degree of participation also had the highest renewal rate and the highest percentage of positive responses to questions regarding commitment to their farm. The members who participated more extensively in their farms experienced greater rewards.

From their conversations with shareholders, Cone and Myhre concluded that for a great many CSA participants, the term "community" referred more to matrix of shared interests than to a community built on mutual relationships of rights and obligations. "Although CSA offers a potential avenue for resistance to food as commodity," they wrote, "it has yet to demonstrate effectiveness in building the sets of stable, committed relationships the movement requires in the long term."

The anthropologists comment that the future success of the CSA movement may depend on the willingness of shareholders to participate more actively in their farms or to pay a higher price for their shares.

Pioneer CSA author Elizabeth Henderson has observed that in general farmers need trust in the community and mutual openness and frankness to take the risk to share their responsibilities with consumers. A John-Wayne, 'I'll-do-it-myself' attitude just doesn't work long-term with a true CSA. As she is quoted in the book *Farmer Jane: Women Changing the Way We Eat*, Henderson observed, "Farmers who do not involve the members of their CSA are missing the social capital, which is amazingly beneficial."

~ *Chapter 3* ~
Three Dormant Seeds

Three seed ideas were among the many elements that underlie the actions of the first CSA farmers who in 1985-86 established new ways of farming in America. Those ways have emerged in subsequent seasons to yield as many as 12,000 contemporary community supported farms in cities, suburbs, towns, villages and churches across the land.

The CSA model has proven to be a natural for adaption and innovation. Many latter-day CSAs, however, have overlooked or bypassed some of the seed ideas as they have established a wide range of variations on the CSA theme. In a sense, those seeds have gone dormant throughout much of the CSA movement. Yet the seeds remain viable, and perhaps may become even more so in our era of profound global change. These embryonic life forms are open pollinated and have no corporate patents pending. Thus as is natural, these seeds are freely available to any individual or community who chooses to plant and cultivate them.

Alice Bennett Groh is part of the 1985-86 founding group for the Temple-Wilton Community Farm, in New Hampshire. Twenty-nine years later, in November 2014, she spoke at a ceremony organized by the Granite State's Peterborough Grange to honor

CSA pioneers. Alice put her focus on three of the seed ideas that helped community farms become established in America and to grow.

With eloquence and economy of language, she told of how her husband Trauger Markus Groh partnered with Anthony Graham and Lincoln Gieger to cultivate new thinking, and thereby to initiate their highly productive, economically sustainable, and environmentally radiant Biodynamic farm on rocky, rolling hills flanking the Souhegan River.

In conversations with me after the historic Grange-CSA event, Alice spoke further about those seed ideas:

First Seed
The first seed that Alice recalled has to do with the ownership and financing of community farms. These are questions Trauger engaged early in his life while living in Germany, questions he engaged again with compatriots at the Temple-Wilton Community Farm, and questions he explored in his autobiography, *Personal Recollections: Remembering My Life and Those Who Mean So Much to Me* (2010).

The general agricultural situation in Germany in the 1960s, according to Trauger and Alice, was that most farms were economically dependent on using foreign workers and paying them low wages. This set up ensured that the farm workers would remain poor and have no stake in the land.

Meanwhile, in comparison with conventional farms where production rose steeply with the addition of synthetic chemical fertilizers, herbicides and insecticides, the financial return from harvests was unsatisfactory for organic and Biodynamic farms.

In this economic and social environment, how could organic or Biodynamic farms survive and prosper into the future? At Buschberg Farm in the 1960s, Trauger and his farm colleagues of that era were all actively cultivating Anthroposophical and Biodynamic understandings based on the work of philosopher Rudolf Steiner. In their discussions at the farm they recognized that new economic, social and agricultural forms were essential.

Understanding that isolated farms and isolated farmers had a dim future in the shadow of corporate-industrial agriculture, they strove to create a wider, village-like arrangement based on free will associations of households with the farm. One great aim was to open the farms to the participation of many people, to share the responsibility of growing food and caring for the earth cooperatively. To make that possible, it was necessary to change the relationship of the ownership to the land, and to give up the conventional employer/employee wage relationship.

They formed a cooperative work group for the Buschberg Farm Agricultural Working Group. The group was composed of about 40 people, with three active farmers including Trauger. Together they bore responsibility for the farm and its risks.

Together they developed a cooperative property association to hold the farmland in trust, and to act as a co-operative credit guarantee company. Attorney Wilhelm Barkoff designed this risk-sharing arrangement in partnership with the Cooperative Bank in Bochum, near Dresden, Germany.

Non-farmer community members worked alongside the active farmers in managing the farm, but did not interfere with it. They contributed to the farm from their own life experience. Each member of the work group was given a loan of 3,000 DM (Deutsche Mark) by the bank. These loans functioned as a line of credit, which the non-farmer members of the community could then assign to the active farmers to give them working capital and enable them to establish a farm budget. The financial and health needs of the active farmers themselves and their families were built into the budget for the farm. Withdrawals were deducted and income credited.

On this basis the active farmers went about their business. If they made a profit they turned it over to the members of whole farm community: if the farm had a loss then the farm community members agreed to make up the difference. They shared the risk. This approach to free will community trust ownership of the land and shared risk was among the original CSA seed ideas.

Second Seed.

While speaking at the Grange ceremony for the pioneers of CSA, Alice told also of how in the 1970s Trauger came to know Peter Berg, a farmer in south Germany. Berg came up with an idea for a box scheme – a weekly box of Biodynamic vegetables for people who wanted them, an approach which he was able to extend to Dornach, across the nearby border with Switzerland.

As a member of the Board of Directors for *Fondation la Bruyére Blanche* and as an agricultural consultant, Trauger visited Dornach many times in the early 1970s, and learned about the approach Berg was taking. Then in the 1980s, an American named Jan Vander Tuin also learned of this approach while visiting in Switzerland. He became passionately enthusiastic. Later when Vander Tuin visited western Massachusetts in 1985, he told about the pre-paid box scheme to a core group of people including John Root, Sr., John Root Jr., Charlotte Zenecchia, Andrew Lorand, and Robyn Van En. They formed The CSA Garden at Great Barrington, later known as Indian Line Farm.

The two communities – Temple-Wilton CSA in New Hampshire and Indian Line CSA in Massachusetts – were less than 150 miles apart. They connected and communicated with each other before the first CSA planting season in America, 1986.

CSA pioneers strove to create organizational forms that would provide direct, free-will support for farm and farmers from the people who eat their food by receiving a share of the harvest they have made possible. This is a second seed idea at the core of CSA.

Third Seed

Alice Groh concluded her talk for the Grange by telling of how in the early 1980s Trauger visited with a farmer named Asgar Elmquist and his wife, Mary. The Elmquists were houseparents at Camphill Village, Copake, New York, and Asgar was also actively farming.

Camphill Villages are set up as households, with food budgets. It was the agreed custom for housemothers to use their budgets to purchase food for all the residents of the households. One option was to buy food for the households from local farmers, such as Asgar. The houseparents were in fact buying from him, but toward the end of each month as house budgets ran low, the housemothers would switch and shop supermarkets instead to save money. That was not working for Asgar because it invariably left him stuck with food that he had produced but could no longer sell while it was fresh.

Asgar proposed that the households pledge a certain amount of budgeted money up front each month to support his general farming efforts, to support the whole farm. In return he would agree to deliver produce to their doors throughout the entire month. That upfront agreement worked better for everyone.

Asgar told Trauger that after he changed over to this arrangement, everything on the farm began to grow better. He explained that the nature spirits, or elemental beings weaving their works in the farm fields, have no relationship to money and no conception of it. If a farmer looks over a row of carrots and principally calculates what money he can earn with them, the elementals cannot grasp this abstraction. But if a farmer is instead thinking about bringing the crop to its highest perfection to nourish human beings and livestock, the elementals can in their own manner comprehend and respond. They have a quality of intelligence particular to their nature.

"Elemental beings want what is good, healthy and right for the soil and the situation," Alice explained. "If a farmer can be freed from the economic stress of counting rows of carrots to calculate how many rows he needs to make how much money, then the farmer can think instead of what the soil, the plants, the farm, and the farm community need. With these thoughts about concrete matters such as food and eating, rather than thoughts about the relatively abstract and artificial concept of money, everything grows better." Careful observation has shown this to be the case.

"We can't see the forces of nature," original Indian Line CSA farmer Hugh Ratcliffe once told me, "but we can see the effects of working consciously with them." Careful observation of nature, and intelligent cooperation with it, are among the great contributions of Biodynamics. And that's how CSA pioneers approached it in the USA.

Considered through the lens of economics, the efforts of CSA pioneers were aimed at the basic economy of freeing farmers to do the tasks that are right for the farm, the people, and the earth. This intention represents a third seed at the core of the original CSA impulse.

The Temple-Wilton Community Farm in particular has taken up these seed ideas from the beginning. With effort it has cultivated and refined the seeds: shared ownership and risk, free-will participation as members of the community, and intelligent partnership with nature.

~ *Chapter 4* ~

Marketing Strategy
or Web of Relationships?

Agrarians have been known to remark in one context or another that they feel farming went off course when people started trying to run farms as a business instead of as a way of life. When that approach took over, some say, farming was no longer a culture of the land, but rather a business of the land — a business that has metastasized over decades to become the modern, genetically modified, chemically fueled behemoth of industrial agribusiness.

As more and more farm enterprises have identified themselves as CSAs, extension services and educators have increasingly described CSA as a business "marketing approach" or "marketing tool." Yet that is the antithesis of what CSA started out to become, and what it still has potential to become. CSA was not initiated in North America as another system to sell food. It was about communities of people directly supporting specific farms, and farms directly supporting specific communities.

There is a creeping risk in our era that CSA could be diverted to a course more devotedly focused on revenue and efficiency in service to profit. But in so doing the movement risks losing its bearings on the matters that were intrinsic to the original concept: agricultural, economical, social, and environmental renewal.

When an enterprise that identifies itself as CSA puts its central focus on profit and comes to regard people as paying consumers, by those very acts has modified the spirit of the movement and morphed into something else – "Genetically Modified CSA," you might say. That something else may be a fabulous business idea that is doing an effective job of fulfilling a real need for consumers and keeping a farm going. That's all admirable. But the business is not a CSA, and the use of CSA as a descriptor for such businesses muddies the picture and undermines the potential of true community supported farms.

To the extent that a "CSA" tends toward a perfunctory vegetables-for-money scheme, it misses the essential spirit and the most promising possibilities of CSA, veering from pathways which may lead toward the fundamental changes that are required.

Over time food corporations have loosely used and thereby eroded the integrity of the term "natural" so that it now has little relevant meaning. Likewise, the meaning of terms like "green" and "sustainable" has changed over the decades, having been compromised, stretched, and in some cases altogether distorted.

The term "CSA" is similarly having its definition eroded. For example, a program description for a 2012 webinar explicitly promoted CSA as a marketing theory: "Generally CSAs work by collecting up-front capital from consumers before the planting season, which buys them a weekly portion of the farm's bounty during the growing months...The basic CSA business model is now a widespread direct-to-consumer marketing strategy."

In a report prepared for the Small Farm Success Project, Lydia Oberholtzer observed that most farmers she interviewed regarded the CSA model as "a good marketing tool." Many of these same farms, however, also reported big challenges, including membership retention, farmer income, and labor. While some CSA farms enjoy high retention rates and long waiting lists of potential members, most are grappling with variations on the loyalty and retention issue.

A food business that does not actively involve the community may be a good and worthwhile enterprise, but it is something else, not a CSA. CSA is not about cheap, convenient food. CSA is about members of the community being responsible, being involved, cooperating, and making a difference.

The USDA defines CSA this way: "CSA consists of a community of individuals who pledge support to a farm operation so that the farmland becomes, either legally or spiritually, the community's farm, with the growers and consumers providing mutual support and sharing the risks and benefits of food production."

The CSA pages for University of Massachusetts-Amherst have long defined CSA in terms of its community dimensions: "Community Supported Agriculture (CSA) is a partnership of *mutual commitment* between a farm and a community of supporters which provides a direct link between the production and consumption of food...Becoming a member creates a responsible relationship between people and the food they eat, the land on which it is grown and those who grow it."

The Biodynamic Farming & Gardening Association defines CSA thusly: "Consumers and farmers work together on behalf of the Earth and each other. While the farmer is tending the Earth on behalf of others, consumers share the costs of supporting the farm and share the risk of variable harvests (and also share the over-abundance of a particularly fruitful years). Membership in the CSA is based on shares of the harvest. Members are called shareholders and they subscribe or underwrite the harvest for the entire season in advance. Each project handles this relationship in its own fashion. Every farm is different in length of season, crops grown, level of social activities and price they set for their shares.

URGENCI, the international network for CSA, offers this explanation: "...growers and eaters... work together to create local social/economic forms, <u>based on trust</u>, encourage initiative and self-reliance, share the risks of agricultural production, share information...(they) are human-scale and efficient, and charge according to needs/costs (not market)."

While many magazines and newspapers pigeonhole CSA as a folksy and colorful new marketing strategy, many other people see something more significant. Anthropologists Cone and Myhre, for example, unhesitatingly identify CSA as a social movement. In their several papers on the subject, they observe that CSA seeks to create a direct relationship between farmers and those who eat their food, the farm shareholders.

Many of the CSA farmers and shareholders they interviewed for their papers saw their commitment to CSA in moral terms. They were dedicated to producing food in an environmentally sustainable manner, and saw themselves as nurturing not just soil and family well being, but also community.

Other CSA observers have also cited the environmental dimension as a motivating factor – families wanting to do something that directly involves them in stabilizing the environment. But Cone and Myhre go deeper. They reference the work of Clifford Geertz in *The Interpretation of Cultures.* He posits that human beings are "suspended in webs of meaning" that they themselves have spun.

"If we follow Geertz's broad definition of religion," Cone and Myhre write, "CSA farms and the food they produce have a religious aspect in that they can serve as symbols of a larger cosmic awareness. Participating in a farm and eating its food thus can potentially transform instrumental activities into ones with ritual significance."

In the book *Modernity and Self-Identity*, Anthony Giddens identifies several dimensions of modernity, including capitalism, industrialism, surveillance by organizations of massive size and scope, and the chronic revision of social relationships in light of new technology and information.

Responding to this, Cone and Myhre wrote, "Research on the perspectives of CSA suggests that this form of agriculture has the potential to solve some of the dilemmas of modernity posed by Giddens. Farmers and shareholders must find a sustainable balance between differing forms of livelihoods and lifestyles that they try to achieve through commitment to shared values..." In concert, these dimensions of modernity tie our personal lives to social connections that are national and global in scope.

Giddens argues that the conditions of modernity create a need for clearly defined community. Extrapolating from this observation, Cone and Myhre reason that when the community dimension is actively cultivated, CSA farms have potential for "re-embedding" people in time and place through linking them to a specific piece of land and to the natural rhythm of the seasons.

"Membership in a farm can offer a connection to the land, to a community, and to a cosmic sensibility that has been lost through the dynamics of modernity," they write. "It is a way to re-embed place and the personal into the self-identity of shareholders, offering them a sense of cohesion with individuals who hold and desire to act on similar ideologies."

CSA tends to bring social realities to the forefront so people can reckon with them. CSA gives participants an avenue to act directly and positively on their social and political values.

~ *Chapter 5* ~
Revisiting *Farms of Tomorrow Revisited*

When Trauger Groh and I coauthored our *Farms of Tomorrow* books on CSA, we offered essays on new structures for farms and communities which advanced the understanding that farming is not just a business like any other profit-making business, but a precondition of all human life on earth, and a precondition of all economic activity. "As such," we wrote, "farming is everyone's responsibility, and has likewise to be accessible for everyone. This fact makes new social structures for farming necessary."

Trauger and I wrote to suggest some possibilities, and also to serve a need that has been becoming increasingly explicit: the need to share the experience of farming with everyone who understands that our relationship with nature and the ways that we use the land will determine the future of the earth.

The problems of agriculture and the environment belong not just to farmers, but are the common problems of all people.

Along with other observers, we saw plainly the staggering problems of pollution, labor exploitation, declining food quality, and health epidemics that have resulted from the industrial model of agriculture. We also saw the redemptive opportunities in directly linking communities with specific, local farms.

A cornerstone idea in *Farms of Tomorrow Revisited* concerns the land. CSAs can and usually do establish environmental oases that radiate their good health out to the wider world not just through the food they produce, but also via the ways they care for and improve the land. Instead of being sources of massive, vexing pollution, CSA farms with their organic, Biodynamic and other agroecological approaches actually work to remediate serious ecological problems and to increase the health, cleanliness and vitality of the natural world.

Farmland cannot continue to be treated as a commodity with an eternally escalating monetary value, the land ever held in a state of debt created by a succession of mortgages. As even the USDA acknowledged as far back as 1938: "mortgages may be as injurious to a farm as erosion or a poor cropping system..." The necessity to appease banks and make mortgage payments has driven hundreds of thousands, if not millions, of farmers from the land. As a consequence, we have far larger industrial-scale farms with far fewer people working and living in proximity.

If communities around the globe are going to be successful in setting a multiplicity of CSAs as cornerstones, they must base their actions on a more intelligent relationship with the land. In Chapter 2 of *Farms of Tomorrow*, Trauger and I set out at length some ideas and propositions that we have seen work well. We posited that over the long term land suitable for agriculture might gradually and steadily be protected by land trusts.

Any selected plot of farmland must be purchased at fair market value for the last time and then – out of the free will initiative of local people – be removed from the market and be placed in forms of trust that will protect it from ever again being mortgaged or sold for the sake of private profit. Non-profit land trusts can then make the farmland available for qualified people to use it. The trusts take land into their legal embrace so that they can serve the basic needs of human beings.

While such an approach to land may initially seem complex, it is actually straightforward and many groups have developed sophisticated understandings of the best ways to accomplish this.

Such changes cannot be successfully initiated or imposed by government, nor should any attempts at political land reform be pursued. History is clear on the pitfalls of that approach. Consequential, wholesale changes in the human relationship with land must arise over time out of the intelligence, free will and free choice of citizens. People must see that it is a good, reasonable and worthwhile thing to arrange to have farmland held in a land trust, and then take action to make it happen.

Transferring the land from private ownership to community ownership via a final, fair-market sale and purchase not only protects the long-term future of the land and the farm, but also allows greater collaboration with the educational, cultural and science sectors of the community than is currently possible and enables the development of more sophisticated facilities on site.

CSA shareholders protect the earth by caring wisely for farmland that produces clean food in a way that is beneficial and that ultimately enriches and heals the land and the waters not just for now, but for generations of our children to come.

~ *Chapter 6* ~
Virtual Community

CSA exists within the wider milieu of the global good-food, community-food movement, which in turn exists intertwined in time and space with the continuing dynamic emergence of a vast, sprawling, high-speed realm of digital information and communication.

In this digital realm, almost since its inception, CSA has been adopting, incorporating and adapting webs of relationship through the wide array of virtual food nodes and farm communities which are networking.

Networks have always existed. What is new is that networks have become the dominant and most fundamental social form of organization in society. This new reality has been made possible by the arrival of mass information and communication technologies.

In the pages of the Sunday *New York Times Magazine*, Jonathan Zittrain, Harvard professor of law and computer science, observed: "The Internet is not merely connecting computers together for the benefit of humans; it's connecting humans together to reinvent labor."

Manuel Castells of the University of California-Berkeley has written about what he terms the emergence of the "network society." In his book *Informationalism and Society* he argues that over the last 20 years the technological paradigm of "informationalism" has replaced industrialism as the dominant paradigm. "A network society," he writes, "is a society whose social structure is made of networks powered by microelectronics-based information and communication technologies."

This kind of pervasive change has social consequences in general, and those consequences naturally bear upon CSAs and other agrarian initiatives.

In response to questions posed by Food+Tech Connect, Beth Hoffman wrote, "For decades technology in agriculture has meant machines and chemicals – bigger combines, stronger pesticides, and genetically engineered seeds. Now, technology based on the sharing of information – data extracted from all points along the food chain – is helping to create a more transparent, equitable, and environmentally sound food system."

In the same survey, Nevin Cohen observed, "The future of agrarianism is not vertical, nor even simply horizontal. It is distributed and networked. In a growing number of cities, suburbs, and small towns, community groups and entrepreneurs have discovered innovative ways to harvest and grow food, using interconnected networks of relatively small plots of public and private land and shared resources. In the process, they are forging novel relationships among producers and consumers."

CSAs and farmers' markets are using social media channels to get the word out about not only what's fresh and available, but also related news and information about the local food movement. Social media such as Facebook and Twitter are playing a significant part in helping these networks form and stay connected. The role of social media and the Internet with the multi-faceted agrarian initiatives of CSA farms will likely become stronger, more sophisticated, and more supportive in the years ahead. What's also been evolving in CSA are matrices of community farms with different capacities and specialties.

~ *Chapter 7* ~
Core Matters

When they studied CSAs extensively at the University of Wisconsin-Madison, John Hendrickson and Marcy Ostrom observed that CSA organizers wanted to strengthen people's connections to their food, its sources, and each other. They noted that as farm members became more committed and involved by helping with organizational tasks and recruiting members, the farmers gained more time to focus their energies and skills on producing high-quality food, caring for their farmland, and caring for themselves and their families.

In *Managing a CSA Farm 2* (Research Brief #41), Hendrikson and Ostrom noted: "Another facet of CSA that strengthens community is the extent to which members are actively involved in either decision-making, food distribution, or administrative tasks." Relationships created through CSAs often create social capital, a type of social resource associated with trust and networks, and useful for purposes beyond the CSA.

The Brief emphasizes the importance of planning and designing volunteer work so that people can give to the farm what they really want to give – whether that involves pulling weeds, boxing vegetables, updating the website, or some other supportive task.

In a report on CSA for the Small Farm Success Project, Lydia Oberholtzer wrote, "Farmers need to pay particular attention to the reasons shareholders join CSA farms when recruiting new members."

In terms of importance, she found that the two highest-rated factors were the desire for fresh, organic, local produce and the opportunity directly to support a local farm. Rating lowest (least likely) reasons for joining a CSA were trying new foods, convenience, less-expensive food, and an opportunity to work on the farm. These results are similar to a number of other surveys. But 50 percent of shareholders in this study said they did not take part in any form of farm activity other than picking up their share.

Many early CSA initiatives incorporated the idea of the core group to help farmers make decisions, gather feedback, and engage members in range of tasks. CSA farms were conceived explicitly with the idea that part of the community's role was to support and help the grower, beyond supporting the whole farm by investing in a share.

In general, a core group is a body of CSA members who agree to take on more responsibility and tasks. A core group does not include the entire CSA membership but usually consists of a handful of people who have a closer relationship with the farmer and/or the farmed land.

Having been part of both structures over the years, I've come to regard CSA core groups as being roughly analogous to the volunteer Boards that manage food co-ops. Co-ops are owned by their members, and each year they elect new owner-members to serve on their Boards, and to help manage the affairs of the co-op through their relationship with the General Manager who runs the enterprise, much as the farmers run the farm. In CSA, core groups can take a similar leadership role in the community of shareholders and have their roles and responsibilities defined in a number of ways, according to the choices of the farm community.

In the realm of community cooperation, core groups stand as an awkward CSA paradox. Many CSA farmers speak of wanting a deeper commitment of farm support from the people in their CSAs, and loyalty over the long term. But core groups of shareholders — a proven loyalty builder — are just not all that popular.

If a core group has a say in the farm, farmers can naturally feel their lives are more complicated, and lots of farmers are looking not for complexity but for simplicity. Thus, core groups do not work for everyone. But when they do work they can accomplish great things.

A core group of volunteers may meet to discuss all manner of things CSA-related, from organizing pickup locations, to managing finances and planning get-togethers. The core group may produce and distribute a weekly newsletter with recipes, news about crops to be harvested, and reminders about volunteer opportunities.

In some cases core groups are responsible for collecting payments, organizing festivals, preparing the budget, paying the farmers, dealing with legal issues, and finding more consumers as required. Other roles can range from setup coordinator, to membership coordinator, events coordinator, managing treasurer, nutrition expert, webmaster, delivery site manager, communications coordinator, community outreach coordinator, and so forth.

Core groups have in many cases been crucial in creating land trust arrangements for specific farms, placing the CSA in a position to enter into a long-term lease for protected land with qualified farmers on negotiated terms.

CSA core groups have the potential — in some cases actualized — to communicate closely with the farmers, to help nail down logistics, and to create dialogue and promote interaction among the shareholders. However, as reported in *CSA Across the Nation*, surveys make it plain that most CSA farms have not been employing this basic CSA element. That's likely still the case.

Core groups have untapped potential for building CSA community at a level beyond what any lone farmer or farm family can accomplish. This reality comes home in the realm of public events such farm visits, field days, planting ceremonies, harvest festivals, potluck suppers, and membership meetings. It's asking a tremendous lot of a farmer or a farm family not only to grow the food, but also to organize and implement that kind of activity year after year. It's generally way too much, especially during the growing season.

Many CSA members appreciate opportunities to plan, organize, and participate in special farm events, even if they are unable to attend. Events with hands-on activities reliably help build strong connections to the farm, and participants in hands-on activities tend to renew their farm memberships reliably. There is something about touching the land, and touching the lives of the farmers farming the land, that rings an authentic note of well being.

On farms with many shareholder volunteers, especially on harvest days, people begin to see how they rely on each other for their food.

To run a CSA successfully, farmers must produce adequate, nutritious and attractive food. That's a baseline. But they and the people around them also have to know how to engage one another creatively and to weave themselves together into a modern community. Cooperation has been a key for those CSAs that have hung together and matured over a number of years.

In the course of their research into CSAs, anthropologists Cone and Myhre observed that while men are frequently key supporters and members of CSA core groups, the bulk of responsibility for CSA development and maintenance, speaking in general terms, has been assumed by women. Their observations led the scholars to question the extent to which the success of the farms depended on the work of women in initiating and maintaining farm membership.

"When we examined the relationship between household composition and participation in farm events," they wrote, "the role of women in supporting CSA farms became even more apparent."

At the time of their studies (1995-2000) the farmers and women shareholders, particularly those who were full- or part-time homemakers, formed the foundation of the burgeoning CSA movement. The CSA participants and their families had an awareness of the benefits of the embededness in the land, in cycles of growth, and in community that CSA can offer.

More recently author Temra Costa made a similar point in broader terms in her book *Farmer Jane: Women Changing the Way We Eat.* Her writing acknowledged formally what anyone close to the scene had to have noticed for some time: "women are driving the sustainable food movement."

This leadership by women in care for the land and the social fabric of the community is noteworthy. By leading the way in helping to establish and to nurture CSAs of radiant environmental health, women are creating community cornerstones that are anchored in something real – land and food – and that can have positive meaning for generations to come.

As colonial refugees and immigrants from Europe and elsewhere swarmed onto the Americas beginning more than 500 years ago, they overlooked one of the key ethical principles that had been followed for millennia by most native peoples, and that was reflected in the pristine quality of the air, the water, and the land. Speaking generally, native traditions tended to respect and honor not just a sky father but also a mother earth. The ethical idea was that both masculine and feminine attributes are important, and for balance they must be both given consideration and expression.

The ethos native to North America explicitly included the feminine dimension of life upon the land. The late Ojibwe elder Art Solomon expressed this indigenous understanding succinctly: *"Woman is the centre of the wheel of life. She is the heartbeat of the people. She is not just in the home, but she is the community, she is in the Nation. Woman is the foundation on which Nations are built."*

In many respects CSA embodies and expresses the original Native American social and environmental ethos often spoken of as the Sacred Hoop. The Sacred Hoop is a metaphor for a core concept, or worldview, encompassing a host of subtleties and paradoxes.

The Sacred Hoop (or "The Circle of Life" in the Disney film, *The Lion King*) represents our interconnectedness with the Earth. It is the understanding that we are in an inevitable web of relationship with minerals, plants, animals, natural forces. As I've come to understand it, a foundational premise of these natural laws is to express respect for all things as part of the Sacred Hoop of Life, and to keep all things in balance, in particular the feminine and masculine qualities and attributes that are integral to life.

Industrial agriculture generally assumes an overall aggressive stance of will power, control and domination in regard to the land and the natural world which gives rise to our food. Industrial agriculture values high efficiency and maximum profit. It also gives rise to imbalance.

The corporate industrial approach tends to be masculine driven to an extreme, and the sheer dominance of this yang approach in the modern world is in some ways analogous to a bird flying with one wing. The bird may beat its wing with furious power, but it will just go round in circles and not make any true progress forward. In fact, the bird (or the industrial system) might do a lot of damage flapping around in such a one-sided, unbalanced manner.

With vision and with both the masculine and the feminine wings activated, working in synchrony, the bird (or the community enterprise) can set a direction and move forward in balance. CSA, via community and intelligent partnership with nature, allows greater natural space for this kind of health and vitality. This is an element of CSA's contemporary reality – and potential future – with roots based in life wisdom that spans the ages.

Walk in Balance
Walk in Beauty

~ *Chapter 8* ~
Shared Risks, Shared Budgets

One important concept woven into the CSA model takes the arrangement beyond the usual commercial transaction: shared risk.

For perhaps most farmers today, the CSA is just one of the ways their produce is marketed. They may also go to the farmers market, sell to restaurants or other institutions, and wholesale. Still, the idea that "we're in this together" remains. On some farms it is stronger than others.

In their *Research Brief #21*, Hendrickson and Ostrom noted that – unlike conventional agriculture, in which farmers bear the risks of weather, pests, and the marketplace alone – in CSA the entire community shares both bounty and scarcity.

The reality of shared risk is a powerful element among the factors that create a sense of community among members, and between members and the farmers, according to Erin Barnett at LocalHarvest.com. If a hailstorm takes out all the peppers, everyone is disappointed together, and together they cheer on the winter squash and the broccoli.

To be truly invested in the CSA, shareholders have a need to see and comprehend the farm's whole budget. CSAs can build commitment and loyalty by being transparent and sharing the full farm budget with shareholder families via the farm's newsletter or website. This gives shareholders a complete understanding of what is going on and what is becoming of the money and labor they have provided to the farm, in addition to all the other activities the farm may be undertaking.

Deeper involvement tends to result in members acknowledging the core realities of their shared enterprise. Shareholders might, for example, come over time to realize that the farmers have no health insurance, and then consider and discuss whether they are willing each to invest perhaps $1 more a week so that health insurance becomes possible. When real life considerations are shared it has a bonding influence.

The more shareholders know about the fiscal realities of a community farm, the more likely and readily the shareholders are to commit themselves.

In their paper *The Social Economy of Rural Reconstruction*, scholars Pan Jia'ena and Du Jieb, employ the concept of "social economy" in reflecting on their experiences in rural reconstruction efforts in Mainland China, focusing on their work with peasant cooperatives and CSA farms.

Synthesizing their experiences, Jia'ena and Jieb

wrote that they came to understand that, as "economic organizations," co-ops and CSAs not only have social goals such as concern for the community, but also their economic character is not a "market economy" divorced from society, but rather what they term a "social economy" that consciously and respectfully includes a community of human beings.

With its primary focus on profit, the market economy tends to divorce social relations from local socioeconomic development. The authors posit that, in contrast, social economies (such as CSAs and coops) are people-centered, community-based, cooperative, and defined by participatory democracy, harmony between the earth and its human inhabitants, and a system of social ownership in which production is not merely for the purpose of consumption, but also to address a range of environmental, economic and social issues.

"In practice," the scholars argue, "the social and the economic can never be clearly separated...Economic problems, which may superficially appear to be independent, are in fact over-determined by all kinds of social and cultural factors, so a holistic perspective of 'social economy' is needed to re-embed the economic into its social context."

"In short," they conclude, "social economy does not serve the accumulation of capital; it is a new model for re-embedding economic development into social relations."

For me this is a key point. The concept of a social economy helps give shape and definition to a model that embeds economic development not into the hands of a few plutocrats or multinational corporations, but rather into the hands of human beings with a web of healthy social relationships that constitute a community. Such are the rewards of a well-run CSA.

CSA pioneers in general conceived of CSAs as both a community effort and a community responsibility. They saw, and began working creatively toward, manifold new social, ecological, economic, and dietary ideals.

CSA was a bold idea, a catalyst for a new economy, as Gary Lamb observed in his landmark 1994 paper, *Community Supported Agriculture: Can it Become the Basis for a New Associative Economy?*

The community farm movement embodies elements of a new associative economy that is fundamentally different from the ruling market economy, Lamb wrote. CSA bears potential for a new, different and healthier social dimension as communities of people come together around essentials: food and land.

When I interviewed Gary for *Farms of Tomorrow*,

he said, "The market economy is driven by the self-interest of every participant. In an associative economy, we associate with our partners – active farmers among themselves, active farmers with all the member households, farm communities with other farm communities. The prevailing attitude is a striving to learn the real needs of our partners, and the ways we can meet them...

"Associative economy means that all participants in the economic process try to listen to the needs of all other partners in the process. The active farmers listen to the needs of the member families. The member families listen to the needs of the farmers. One community farm associated with the other community farms in a bioregion listens to the needs of the others. On this basis they proceed."

As we have learned from experience, CSA works best with an active and involved community, a group of people intent upon cooperating for both personal and group goals. This attitude – putting people at the heart of one's efforts – is the basis of associative economy, and associative economics with its social dimension was the theoretical basis of CSA.

One cannot regard CSA's social and environmental dimensions as distinct from the economic element. They are interwoven.

In Gary Lamb's book *Associative Economics: Spiritual*

Activity for the Common Good, he wrote, "associative economics is concerned with and depends on building and sustaining healthy relationships."

Indeed, the precepts of associative economics as derived from Rudolf Steiner's indications, describe what emerged to become the core mission of CSA farms: economic arrangements that foster fair and healthy interaction among producers, traders, and consumers, and where appropriate price, true human needs, greater social equity, and environmental benefits are explicitly addressed in the process.

The key economic question for a CSA that is expressing associative economics, either explicitly or implicitly, is not "How can we make a monetary profit?" Rather the several questions are "What does the farm need? What do the farmers need? What do the shareholders need?" In response to these questions, the community proceeds in its work.

As Lamb wrote: "The most basic necessity of earthly life - food - can provide the starting point for moving from our present government-guided, production-driven market economy, which is based on competition, to an independent associative economy based on consumer needs and conscious, rational decisions between producers and consumers."

~ *Chapter 9* ~
Conflict Resolution

In the early 1980s I was introduced to the principles of Biodynamic farming and gardening by a next-town neighbor, Lincoln Gieger. Lincoln is a founder, and the dairyman for the Temple-Wilton Community Farm in New Hampshire, and an all-around accomplished land steward and philosopher. Holding class in his farm kitchen, Lincoln advocated that one of the first and foremost tasks for farmers or gardeners was to define and protect the boundaries by setting fences. This is farm, this is not. This is garden, this is not. Setting boundaries tends to make subsequent farm and garden decisions clearer and more manageable because they are defined.

In antiquity, Greek mathematician Pythagoras (570–495 BCE) posited the notion, "Limits give form to the Limitless," a Saturnian postulation that plays out in our world's geometry and geography, as well as on our farms.

In the realm of human relationships, likewise, within the complex context of the personalities participating in a community farm, well-defined limits or boundaries can help ensure harmony in long-term associations, and create circumstances conducive to bringing out the best in each person. When consciously agreed upon out of free will, limits can establish incubators for CSA creativity and prosperity. Things have to be conscious. Things have to be honestly brought forward.

In *Farms of Tomorrow*, Trauger wrote "...while we surely enter or create a community bringing in our ideals, at the same time we also bring in our lower nature, containing unhealthy ambition, jealousy, greed, carelessness, and so forth. These elements of our nature can easily undermine or wreck the community if we do not have a clear, accepted structure."

CSAs are well advised to establish ways to handle the likelihood of social disharmonies, such as fundamental disagreements among the active farmers, or between the farmers and the supporting farm community, and between the farm community and the landowners. While not inevitable, disagreements and personality conflicts are common in almost every human community.

Indeed, over the last three decades a great number of CSAs have waned because of the inability of the people involved to get along with one another. Disagreements can, of course, burn up vast quantities of time, energy, and good will. Indian Line Farm in Massachusetts, as one example, had a difficult split in its early days. The pioneer CSA farm started out in the late 1980s with a substantial list of ideals, including fair pay for workers, sustainable care for the land, plants and animals, to be energy conscious and efficient, and to support community control of the land. Most of those initial ideals have remained intact. But along the way, in the early years, the community ran into some sharp philosophical differences that it needed to engage and resolve.

Disagreements arose in three general areas: determining who has how much decision-making authority, determining the role of the shareholders in the CSA, and the relative importance of Biodynamic farming techniques versus general organic farming techniques. The community also faced disagreements on the matter of acquiring land.

Such conflicts can and do arise in most human enterprises. Yet, if skillfully resolved within the CSA, the conflicts can lead to positive learning, maturation, and growth.

CSA author Elizabeth Henderson (*Sharing the Harvest*) recommends that community farms establish a formal conflict resolution process. Such a process, she has written, is part of making CSA sustainable. The group must have a way to resolve the differences that are sure to come up. Whoever is involved in disagreements should be able to readily access a process for sitting and talking and negotiating, or if necessary engaging a mediator either from inside or outside the CSA.

One approach to handling CSA disharmonies is for the participants to agree in writing at the beginning to establish an arbitration board and to agree, likewise in writing, to follow the ruling of this board.

When somebody's rights have been violated, there needs to be a group process for dealing with this, perhaps restorative justice, or a similar form. Restorative justice is a process where all stakeholders affected by an injustice have an opportunity to discuss how they have been affected by the injustice and to decide what should be done to repair the harm.

~ *Chapter 10* ~

The Quintessence
of Community Intelligence

Possessing a substantial array of beneficial and egalitarian dimensions, CSA can continue to establish 21st Century agrarian models with wide, positive implications for decades to come. CSA represents a significant departure from the hierarchical systems of feudalism and capitalism, and establishes instead social and economic relations based on free-will networks of formal association. That's a very different kind of thing. But the qualities of different, intelligent and creative are absolutely necessary to address our prevailing environmental, economic and social circumstances.

CSAs are metaphorical, metaphysical and material systems that through their community networks can and do establish clean, stable agrarian cornerstones for the high-speed, high-tech digital-wave culture which is continuing its energetic emergence – a digital culture which can in reciprocity connect, network and sustain the agrarian initiatives which give it roots.

Ultimately, community is as essential to the success of a CSA as healthy soil and skilled farmers. But to fulfill their role with CSA successfully, communities must have their intelligence awakened and they must step willingly into action.

As CSA farmer John Peterson of Angelic Organics once told me, "A farm is not just an economic unit to produce food. It's also a living social, environmental and educational organism." Now is the time when, in consideration of global conditions, many millions need to realize this, and then to lead their communities forward in clean, healthy sustainable directions.

To bring the community dimension of CSA into greater maturity, and to more fully network CSAs in specific, geographic regions, is a task that calls for the active involvement of citizens who choose of their own free will to become CSA shareholders. It's too much to ask the active farmers to carry that additional responsibility on their own. Ultimately, each community must activate and cultivate itself. This opportunity requires acts of both individual and collective will.

CSAs and food co-ops have in general demonstrated a capability to address and meet a *triple bottom line* of economics, environment, and community in qualitative ways beyond the capacity of profit-focused corporations or farms. This is community intelligence in action.

The dynamic of farmers and consumers sharing interactions, experiences and risks in a CSA – in relation to matters as central as land and food – creates healthy conditions for the further development of community intelligence. Community intelligence is something essential to our long-term prosperity and democracy.

A CSA that has evolved to become a cornerstone for a community of human beings – whether in an urban block, a suburban neighborhood, a reservation, a church or temple, or workplace – orients the people and their resources in a healthy manner, creating a point of substantive connection with the land as global culture reckons with ongoing financial, climatological, social and political permutations.

CSA farms have potential to bridge the gap between the personal and the global. In so doing they convey to shareholders the elements of an authentic and dignified identity as human beings who are consciously and actively part of a community that is anchored and oriented on a specific plot of nearby farmland, with a tangible connection to the natural cycles of life. In this manner the people contribute not just to their family's and community's health and well-being, but they also have a wider global impact as a node of environmental and human health consciously woven into a network of associations.

Indeed, CSAs are *Not Just About Vegetables,* as Robyn Van En opined so memorably three decades ago. Likewise, CSAs are *Not Just About Equitable Economics* nor are they *Just About A Clean Environment*, or a *Healthy Diet.* For certain CSA involves all this, but it's also about far more. CSA shines as a model for re-embedding economic development into healthy social and environmental relationships. In our era of accelerated environmental peril, that is community intelligence in action.

As I hear it, *the call of the land* in regard to CSA farms has to do with hundreds of thousands of communities of people coming together in creative, positive response to the challenges of our era. CSAs can serve as dynamic yet durable cornerstones that will help sustain the lives of millions of humans expressing themselves in the infinite number of ways to which the human spirit is inclined.

While CSA is not the full answer to the world's many crises, it is one proven and worthwhile modern agrarian response at this juncture of the 21st Century. Community Supported farms are material, metaphorical and metaphysical cornerstones that can be laid in the context of a wide variety of communities, congregations, co-ops and corporations. From this, over more than three decades, good has come. Much more good can arise in the decades and centuries ahead. That would be the quintessence of community intelligence. Now is the time for it to be awakened.

Cornerstone detail, temple of Pharoh Khafre, Nile Valley, Egypt.
(Photo by Keith Payne, Wikimedia Commons)

 *End*

BIBLIOGRAPHY

Barnett, Erin, series of articles on CSA published on the *Local Harvest* website, localharvest.org

Bougherara, D., G. Grolleau, and N. Mzoughi. 2009. *Buy Local, Pollute Less: What Drives Households to Join a Community Supported Farm?* Ecological Economics 68:1488-1495.

Carver, John and Miriam. FAQ about the Policy Governance Model, Accessed May 8, 2012, carvergovernance.com

Castells, M. (2004). *Informationalism, Networks, And The Network Society: A Theoretical Blueprint.* In Castells, M. (Ed.), The Network Society: A Cross-Cultural Perspective. Northampton, MA: Edward Elgar.

Cone, Cynthia Abbott, and Andrea Myhre. *Community-Supported Agriculture: A Sustainable Alternative to Industrial Agriculture?* Human Organization, Vol. 59, No. 2, 2000, Society for Applied Anthropology.

Cone, Cynthia Abbott and Kakaliouras, Ann. *Community Supported Agriculture: Building Moral Community or an Alternative Consumer Choice.* Culture & Agriculture. Spring/Summer 1995. pp 28-31.

Cone, Cynthia Abbott, and Ann Kakaliouras. *The Quest for Purity, Stewardship of the Land, and Nostalgia for Sociability: Resocializing Commodities through Community Supported Agriculture.* CSA Farm Network: Volume II,

Stillwater, N.Y.: CSA Farm Network, 1995.

Costa, Temra. *Farmer Jane: Women Changing the Way We Eat.* Gibbs Smith, 2010, Layton, Utah.

Curtis, Kynda R., Associate Professor and Food and Agricultural Marketing Specialist, Department of Applied Economics. *Direct Marketing Local Foods: Differences in CSA and Farmers' Market Consumers,* Economics/Applied Economics, Utah State University - Extension, 2011.

DeLind, Laura B., and Anne Ferguson. *Is this a Woman's Movement? The Relationship of Gender in Community Supported Agriculture in Michigan.* Human Organization 58: 190-200. 1999.

Etzioni, Amitai. *A Moderate Communitarian Proposal.* Political Theory 24: 155-171. 1996.

Food+Tech Connect, *Leading Food and Technology Innovators on 'Hacking' the Food System* Series. In October, 2011 Food+Tech Connect asked leading food and technology innovators – how can information and technology be used to hack the food system? foodtechconnect.com

Good Food Network. *The Five Top Farm Pages* on Facebook. goodfoodmediagroup.com

Geertz, Clifford, *The Interpretation of Cultures*. 1973. New York: Basic Books.

Giddens, Anthony. *Modernity and Self-Identity: Self and Society in the Late Modern Age.* Stanford University Press, 1991.

Greer, L. (1999). *Community Supported Agriculture.*

Business Management Series. Fayetteville, AR: Appropriate Technology Transfer for Rural Areas (ATTRA).

Groh, Trauger and McFadden, Steven. *Farms of Tomorrow Revisited: Community Supported Farms, Farm Supported Communities*. Kimberton, PA: The Biodynamic Farming and Gardening Association, Inc. 1998.

Henderson, Elizabeth, and Robyn Van En. *Sharing the Harvest: A Citizen's Guide to Community Supported Agriculture*. Chelsea Green, White River Junction, Vermont. Rev. and expanded ed. 2009.

Hendrickson, John and Ostrom, Marcy. *Managing a CSA Farm 2: community, economics, marketing and training*. Research Brief #41, March 1999, Center for Integrated Agricultural Systems (CIAS).

Hendrickson, John, and Ostrom, Marcy. *Community Supported Agriculture: Growing Food and Community*. Research Brief #21, October 1996, Center for Integrated Agricultural Systems, University of Wisconsin - Madison.

Jia'ena and Jieb, Du. *The Social Economy of New Rural Reconstruction. China Journal of Social Work* - Vol. 4, No. 3, November 2011, 271–282

Lamb, Gary. *Community Supported Agriculture: Can it become the Basis of a New Associative Economy?* 1994. Threefold Review 11: 39-44.

Lamb, Gary. *The Fundamental Social Law: Theory and Practice*, by Gary Lamb. *Biodynamics,* Spring, 2008.

Lamb, Gary. *Associative Economics: Spiritual Activity for the*

Common Good. AWSNA Publications, 2010.

Lang, K.B. 2005. *Expanding Our Understanding of Community Supported Agriculture (CSA): An Examination of Member Satisfaction*. Journal of Sustainable Agriculture 26(2):61-79.

Lass, Daniel, and Stevenson, GW. *CSA Across the Nation: Findings from the 1999 Survey*. Center for Integrated Agricultural Systems College of Agricultural Life Sciences, University of Wisconsin-Madison (2003).

Lawrence, Robert (Shannon, Kerry; McKenzie, Shawn). *Food System Policy, Public Health and Human Rights in the United States*, published Spring, 2015 in the *Annual Review of Public Health*.

Ludt, Matt, board River Market in Stillwater, Minnesota. *Telling Our Story: What Do the Members Think?* March 2012 newsletter of CDS Consulting Corp. cdsconsulting.coop

Macias, Thomas. *Working Toward a Just, Equitable, and Local Food System: The Social Impact of Community-Based Agriculture*. Social Science Quarterly Volume: 89, Issue: 5, (2008).

McFadden, Steven. *The Call of the Land: An Agrarian Primer for the 21st Century*, 2nd ed. NorLights Press, 2011.

McFadden, Steven. *Community Farms at the Turn of the Millennium: Outside the Box, But Inside the Hoop*. Article. Chiron Communications, 2001. Chiron-communications.com

National Good Food Network webinar on CSA Marketing, May 14, 2012. ngfn.org

Oberholtzer, Lydia. *Community Supported Agriculture in the Mid-Atlantic Region: Results of a Shareholder Survey and Farmer Interviews,* July, 2004.

Poppen, Jeff. *Community Supported Agriculture and Associative Economics.* Biodynamics, Spring 2008.

Practical Farmers of Iowa online seminar with CSA author Elizabeth Henderson, March 15, 2011. practicalfarmers.org.

Sharp, Jeff ; Imerman, Eric; and Peters, Greg. *Community Supported Agriculture (CSA): Building Community Among Farmers and Non-Farmers.* June 2002, Volume 40, Number 3. Journal of Extension.

Steiner-Adair, Catherine and Barker, Teresa H. *The Big Disconnect: Protecting Childhood and Family Relationships in the Digital Age.* Harper, 2013.

Steiner, Rudolf, *Towards Social Renewal*, Rudolf Steiner Press, 1977. http://wn.rsarchive.org/Books/GA023/English/SCR2001/GA023_index.html

UMass-Amherst Extension. CSA definition on their website "North American Community Supported Agriculture." extension.umass.edu

Usher, Stephen E. *The Threefold Social Organism: An Introduction.* www.rudolfsteinerweb.com

Van En, Robyn. *It's not just about vegetables.* Video about CSA, 1986.

Zittrain, Jonathan. Harvard professor of law and computer science quoted in *The New York Times Magazine,*

Sunday, June 3, 2012.

ABOUT THE AUTHOR

Author photo by Elizabeth Wolf (2015)

Independent journalist Steven McFadden has been writing about CSA farms since their inception in America in 1986. With Trauger Groh he is co-author of the first two books on CSA: *Farms of Tomorrow: Community Supported Farms, Farm Supported Communities* (1990) and *Farms of Tomorrow Revisited* (1998). He's also the author of *The Call of the Land: An Agrarian Primer for the 21st Century*--and *Deep Agroecology: Farms, Food, and Our Future (2019).*

Steven's other non-fiction books include: *Profiles in Wisdom*; *Teach Us To Number Our Days*; *Legend of the Rainbow Warriors*; *A Primer for Pilgrims*; *Tales of the Whirling Rainbow*, and *Classical Considerations*.

He's the author of a contemporary, epic, nonfiction saga of North America that is freely available online: *Odyssey of the 8th Fire* < 8thfire.net >.

WEB SITES

Lightandsoundpress.com

chiron-communications.com

DeepAgroecology.net

8thFire.net

SELECTED REVIEWS

Journal of Agriculture, Food Systems, and Community Development: "...Readers new to this movement sometimes struggle to identify a primer that is accessible and grounded in real-world examples. *The Call of the Land* lends itself as a tool for such readers, as it not only illustrates a foundational agrarian ethos historically argued by Wendell Berry and Wes Jackson, but it also outlines a variety of practical models and approaches to inform the practice of local food system development."

Resurgence Magazine about *Farms of Tomorrow*: "It is rare to come across any practical farming guide that sets out, from its inception, a set of principles that embrace social, spiritual and economic concerns on completely equal terms...The wisdom and clarity of philosophy are striking throughout."

Whole Earth Review about *Farms of Tomorrow*: "This is the best book to access the Community Supported Agriculture (CSA) movement, including philosophical, spiritual, practical essays and how-to (including financial discussions). This is the source for tools, organizations, farms, and networks concerning the renewal of agriculture."

Independent Publisher about *The Call of the Land*: "The ecology of our planet and the health of its inhabitants is in peril, because we've lost our connection to the land. This book describes how we can rally to save the quality of our air, water and soil through a new agrarian revolution — starting at the local level to regain control of our food supply — and bring back a sane, intelligent, and holistic approach to the way we live on the land. Steven McFadden describes with eloquence and detail how it's already underway across the continent, and his book is a cornucopia of resources and ideas..."

Courtney White, Director, the Quivira Coalition, author of *Revolution on the Range: The Rise of a New Ranch in the American West: "The Call of the Land* is an important and timely primer on a resurgent agrarianism taking place around the nation. As the challenges of the 21st Century begin to bear down, we can take solace, and find pragmatic solutions, in the back-to-the-land work of progressive farmers, ranchers, conservationists, and many others. Hope dwells in the grassroots. This book is a great guide on where to look."

Farmer John Peterson, Angelic Organics "In the face of widespread turmoil and resignation, *The Call of the Land* shows us that our hands, minds, and hearts, when used as one, are already healing ourselves and the planet earth. Author Steven McFadden reminds us that the seeds to a new future are being planted right now..."

Ingrid Kirst, Director of Community CROPS: *"The Call of the Land* will inspire you with page after page of innovative projects across the country that are having a positive impact on how we eat. Explore this comprehensive list of positive ideas and then implement them in your own community."

Charles Francis, UNL Center for Sustainable Agricultural Systems: "McFadden's call to action is clearly written and well referenced with a robust list of current websites and a bibliography for general reading on positive methods for resolving our food security challenge. Anyone interested in a good contemporary overview of challenges and solutions will find the book valuable."

New York Times Book Review: *"Profiles in Wisdom* does a fine job not only of presenting the dignity, complexity, and wit of important Indian philosophers and religious leaders, but also of issuing cautions against easy uplift and wisdom injections...There are some stirring and unexpected powers unleashed in this book."

Odyssey Magazine about *Legend of the Rainbow Warriors*: "I urge everyone on the spiritual path to read this small yet exceptionally powerful book."

Library Journal about *Profiles in Wisdom:* "This wise and provocative collection is highly recommended."

Headline Muse about *Legend of the Rainbow Warriors*: "In the wake of the September 11 tragedies, *The Legend of the Rainbow Warriors* is of added import. Clearly, human existence is experiencing profound shifts of consciousness...As one struggles to make sense of these recent events McFadden offers substantive insight and hope. Further, he speaks to the power of individuals to address the overwhelming and complex problems facing us today—locally as well as globally."

The Washington Times about *Profiles in Wisdom*: "Our leaders should sit and listen to the counsel Steven

McFadden has gathered in this book."

Critique Magazine: "To the uninitiated, reading Steven McFadden's *Legend of the Rainbow Warriors* is a bit like hearing one's native language spoken with an entirely new accent. The words are familiar, and the ideas and events of which he writes are certainly not news. But the light Mr. McFadden uses to illuminate his subject is alien. Self-sacrifice and stewardship of the land do not mix well with the American traditions of further, faster, and damn the consequences. Indeed, the juxtaposition of American-style progress and Native American sensibilities is one of history's oddest coincidences..."

Soul*Sparks Books

Soul*Sparks Books is an imprint of Light and Sound Press, LLC, an independent venture of married partners Elizabeth Wolf and Steven McFadden.

As an independent enterprise we are self-directed and self-governing. We are free of affiliation with any organization, government, religion, financial institution, or other entity.

As publishers we are salutary. By that we mean our intentions and actions are focused on supporting healthy improvement in the natural environment, as well as in the realm of human development.

The word "spark" conveys the idea of something small but active, exciting, and filled with potential and spiritual fire. That's the basic editorial and artistic vision that we hold for the Soul*Sparks series of gift books.

The books in the Soul*Sparks series published by Light and Sound Press strive to deliver insight and inspiration on popular themes through reports and essays by the authors, as well as excerpts from visionary writers, thinkers, artists, and spiritual savants.

~ Other Soul*Sparks Titles ~

Tales of the Whirling Rainbow:
Myths & Mysteries for Our Times

Native Knowings
Wisdom Keys for One and All

Classical Considerations: Musings Prompted
by the Late Harvard Master John H. Finley

Keys for Adept Aging

A Primer for Pilgrims

Soul*Sparks Books
An imprint of Light and Sound Press
Albuquerque, *New Mexico USA*

lightandsoundpress.com